To:_____

From:_____

Date:_____

The Jesus With Us Series is dedicated to showing children how much He loves them and that He is always with them. This awareness will develop faith and confidence, paving the way for a brighter future.
— S&L

Copyright © 2022 by Sybrand & Lucia. All rights reserved.
Published by Ciana Publishers.

This Book is Copyright Protected:
This is only for personal use. You cannot amend, distribute, sell, use, quote, or paraphrase any part of the content within this book without the consent of the authors. The Authors guarantee all contents are original and do not infringe upon the legal rights of any other person or work.

No part of this book may be reproduced, duplicated, or transmitted in any form by means such as printing, scanning, photocopying, or otherwise, without direct written permission from the authors or publisher, except for the use of quotations in a book review and as permitted by the U.S. copyright law. For permission, contact info@cianapublishers.com.

Disclaimer and Terms of Use:
This book is provided solely for spiritual upliftment, entertainment, motivational and informational purposes.

All Scripture quotations, unless otherwise indicated, are taken from the Holy Bible, New International Version®, NIV®. Copyright ©1973, 1978, 1984, 2011 by Biblica, Inc.™ Used by permission of Zondervan. All rights reserved worldwide. www.zondervan.com The "NIV" and "New International Version" are trademarks registered in the United States Patent and Trademark Office by Biblica, Inc.™

Authors - Sybrand JvR & Lucia S

cianapublishers.com

THE RHYME OF THE GOOD SAMARITAN IS BASED ON LUKE 10:25-37

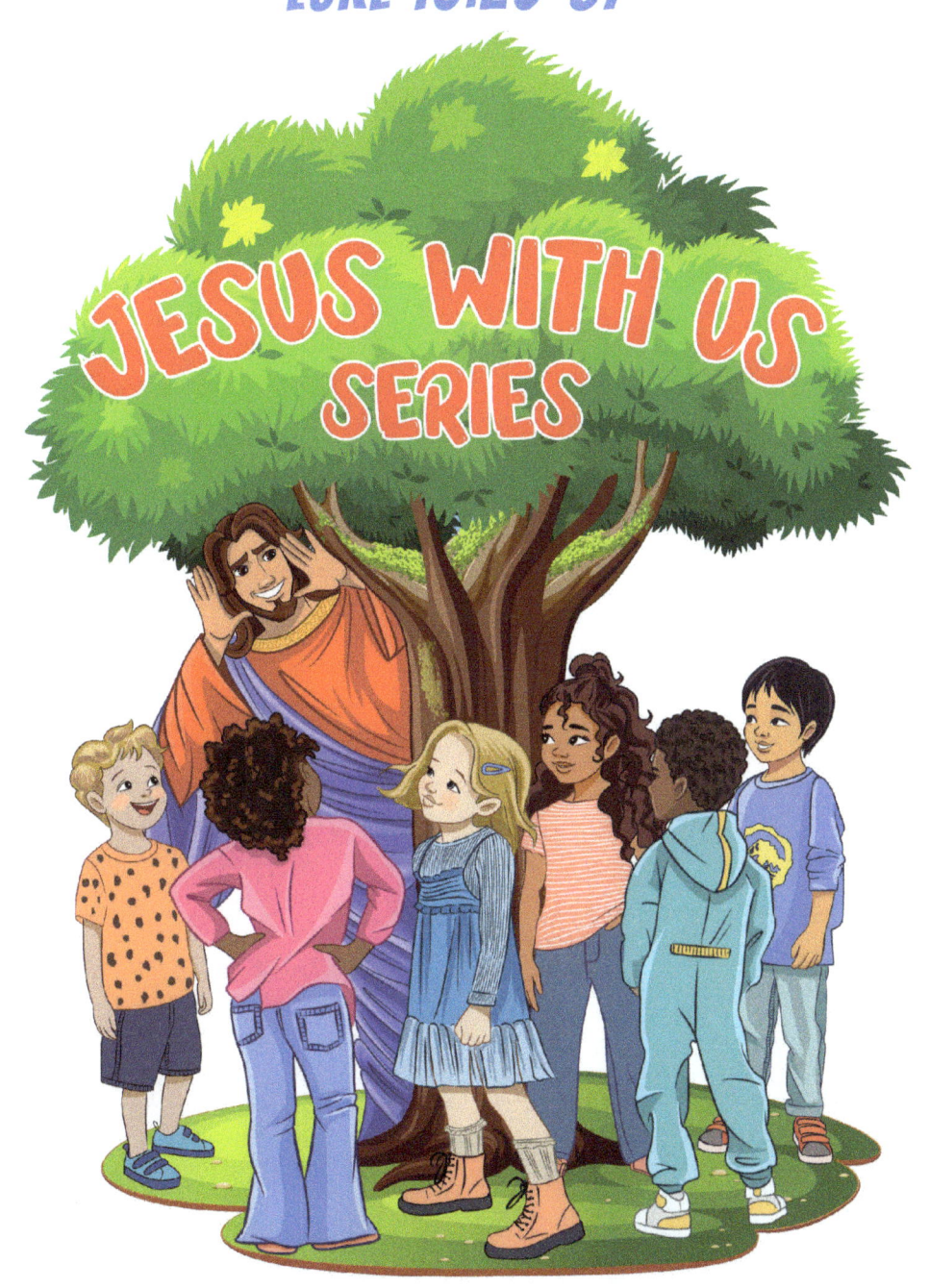

From Jerusalem to Jericho, a lone man went.
Smiling and happy, and totally content.
Not an ordinary guy but a well-to-do gent.

Robbers on the road made the day turn black.
They jumped on the man, "We're here to attack."
"Give us your money; there's no turning back."

They took his clothes, and then they fled.
The poor man lies on the street, half dead.
With gashes and bruises all over his head.

In a foetal position, holding his knees.
In tears and pain, and not at ease.
Silently praying, "Lord help me, please."

A Levite came by and saw the man's plight.
"It looks like he's been in a terrible fight."
"It's better for me to stay out of sight."

A Samaritan saw the wounded, and he took pity.
Moved with compassion; the scene wasn't pretty.
"I have to make haste and get him to the city."

He bandaged his wounds with oil and wine.
"It hurts my heart as you're not doing fine."
"I'll treat you like a brother of mine."

"Helping you gives me joy inside."
"I'll put you on my donkey to ride."
"Don't worry; I'm here to provide."

He took him to the nearest inn.
"Here, your recovery will begin."
"From today, you're my next of kin."

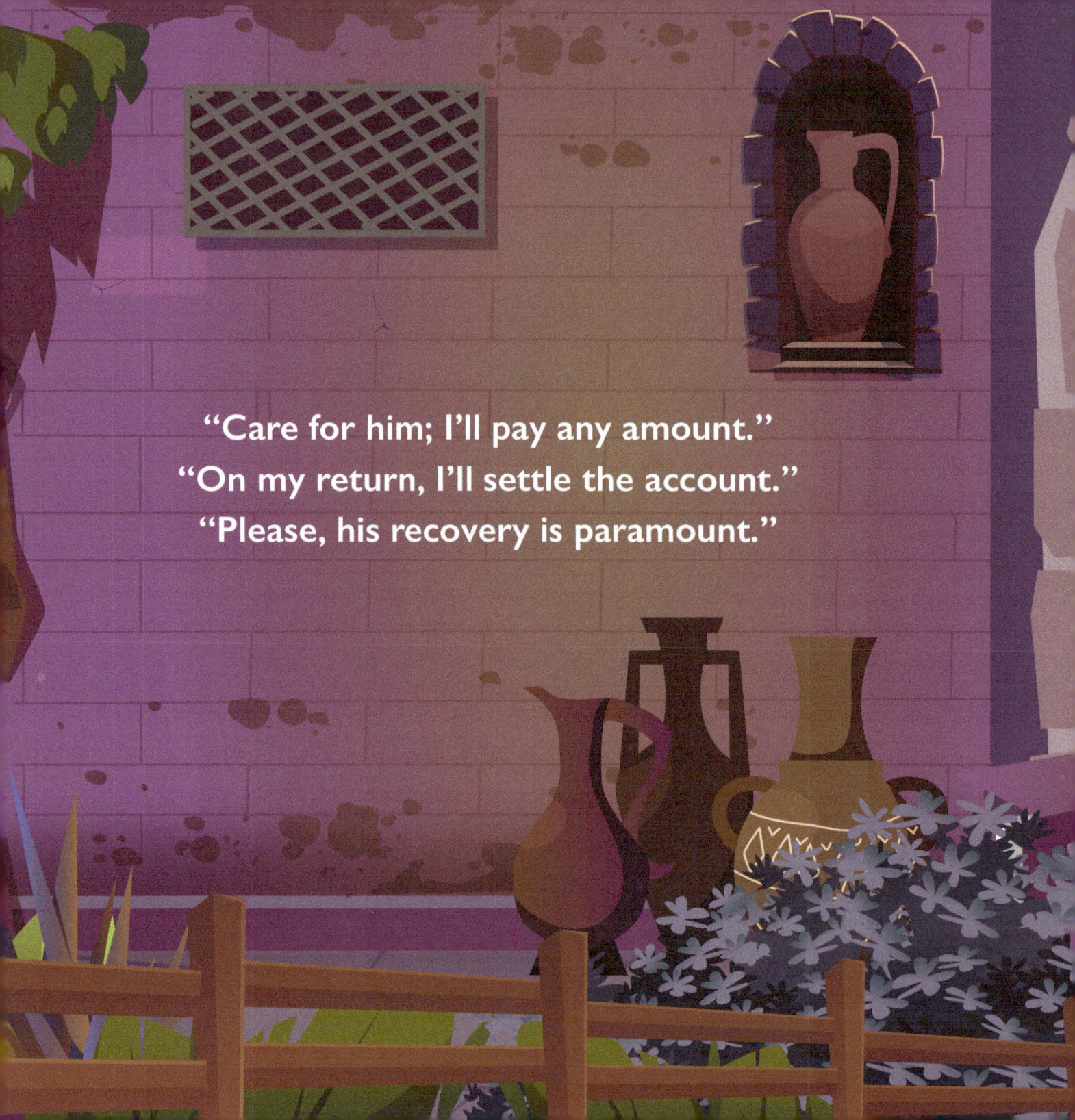

"Care for him; I'll pay any amount."
"On my return, I'll settle the account."
"Please, his recovery is paramount."

Praise the Lord!
Everyone has something to give. You, too, have something to give. Ask yourself, "As young as I am, what do I have to give?"

It could be your smile, your time, your greeting, your kindness, or your help. It could be your advice or to cheer someone up.

The Good Samaritan helped the man, yet he had many reasons not to. He didn't wait for someone else to do good before doing it himself. Don't wait to be helped before you help. Don't wait to receive before you give. When you remember the times you were helped, you will be quick to help.

Ask Jesus to give you His eyes so you can see those who are in need of what you have to give. Ask Him to give you His ears so you can hear the cries of those who are in need of what you have to give.

Tell somebody. "Be the Difference."

Dear Jesus.

Thank you for all Your care.
And for all I have to share.

Give me Your eyes to see those in need.
And grace to make a difference as I plant a seed.

In Jesus' name.

Amen! Amen! Amen!

LUKE 10:30-34 NIV

30 In reply, Jesus said: "A man was going down from Jerusalem to Jericho, when he was attacked by robbers. They stripped him of his clothes, beat him and went away, leaving him half dead.

31 A priest happened to be going down the same road, and when he saw the man, he passed by on the other side.

32 So too, a Levite, when he came to the place and saw him, passed by on the other side.

33 But a Samaritan, as he traveled, came where the man was; and when he saw him, he took pity on him.

34 He went to him and bandaged his wounds, pouring on oil and wine. Then he put the man on his own donkey, brought him to an inn, and took care of him.

FOR FURTHER READING: LUKE 10:25-37

LET'S CHAT

Name three things The Good Samaritan did to show kindness. _____
_____
_____

What can you say about the behaviours of the Priest and the Levite? _____
_____
_____

When a friend cries, do you wait to see if anyone else helps before finding out what is wrong?
_____
_____

Do you think it is easy or difficult to greet, smile, or cheer someone up, and why do you say so? _____
_____

Do you agree that everyone has something to give? _____
_____
_____

As young as you are, what do you have to give?_____
_____
_____

Name a few things you can thank Jesus for. _____
_____
_____

WORDS IN THE RHYME MADE EASY TO UNDERSTAND

Parables:
Stories told by Jesus to teach us how to be good and to tell us more about His Kingdom, His Father, and Heaven.

Content:
In the rhyme, 'content' means, 'Someone who is at peace and happy with what they have.'

Gashes:
In the rhyme, 'gashes' means, 'Long, deep cuts and wounds on the wounded man's body.'

Foetal position:
A position in which someone lies on their side, making a C-shape, with their knees pulled up to their chest.

Priest:
In Biblical times, a 'priest' was set apart for the service of God and a teacher of God's Word. In the rhyme, the priest was expected to help the wounded man.

Levite:
In Biblical times, a 'Levite' did different chores in the church and worked with the priests. In the rhyme, the Levite was expected to help the wounded man.

Plight:
In the rhyme, 'plight' means, 'The man was in a very bad situation after being attacked, with gashes and bruises all over his head.'

Samaritan:
In Biblical times, a 'Samaritan' was someone who came from the country Samaria. The Samaritan was the least expected person to help the wounded man. Nowadays, a person who helps someone in need is called a 'Good Samaritan.'

Compassion:
In the rhyme, 'compassion' means, 'To feel what someone else feels. Their pain is your pain, and their trouble is your trouble.'

WORDS IN THE RHYME MADE EASY TO UNDERSTAND

Provide:
In the rhyme, 'provide' means, 'A person who helps someone. It can be by giving food, money, their smile, time, greeting, kindness, or help.'

Inn:
In the rhyme, 'inn' means, 'It is like a small hotel or Bed & Breakfast which provides food and accommodation for travellers.'

Next of kin:
In the rhyme, 'next of kin' means, 'The Good Samaritan tells the wounded man that he is like family to him.'

Denarii:
'Denarii' are coins that were used as money in Biblical times.

Don't despair:
In the rhyme, The Good Samaritan says to the wounded man, "don't despair." This means, 'Don't worry because I will take care of everything.'

Paramount:
Something very important.

Settle the account:
In the rhyme, 'settle the account' means, 'The Good Samaritan agrees to pay for the wounded man's bill at the inn, for his stay, food, and care.'

Be the difference:
In the message, 'Be the Difference' means, 'Make a positive change in someone's life by doing good. As one of Jesus' children, do what Jesus would do in the lives of others.'

Grace:
In the prayer, 'grace' means, 'Although I don't deserve it, please help me and strengthen me to plant a seed.' Also, read (Ephesians 2:8).

Plant a seed:
In the prayer, 'plant a seed' means, 'Doing something good for someone that makes a positive change in their life.'

OTHER BOOKS IN THE JESUS WITH US SERIES

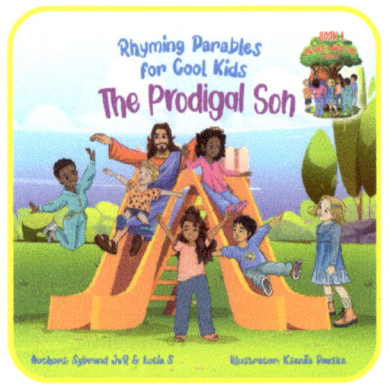 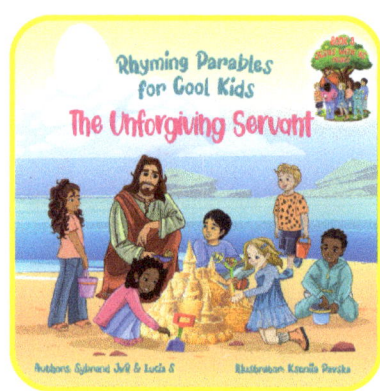 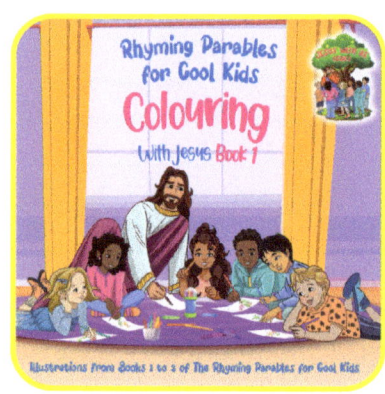

SCAN ME

OTHER BOOKS BY THE AUTHORS

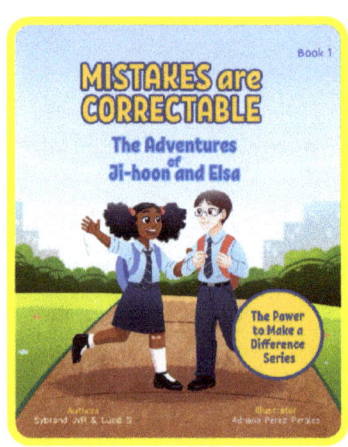 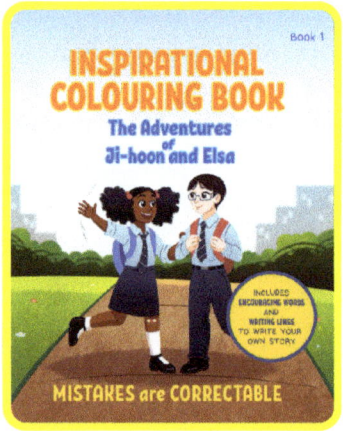